The making of the

Finest Hour

Winston S. Churchill

The making of the
Finest Hour

18 June 1940

Introduction by Richard M. Langworth CBE

LEVENGER
PRESS

Delray Beach, Florida

Published by Levenger Press
420 South Congress Avenue
Delray Beach, Florida 33445 USA
800.544.0880
Levengerpress.com

ISBN-13: 978-1-929154-26-5
ISBN-10: 1-929154-26-7

CD produced in the USA
Text printed and bound in Mexico

Cover and book design by Danielle Furci
Mim Harrison, Editor

Contents

*Page numbers on the first draft skip from 3 to 5

Acknowledgments

Levenger gratefully acknowledges Mr. Winston S. Churchill's generosity in granting us access to this speech, and for entrusting us to honor his grandfather with a book that we hope generations will enjoy.

Our thanks to Lady Soames and Minnie Churchill; to Allen Packwood, Andrew Riley and Sandra Marsh of the Churchill Archives Centre; to Judith Seaward and Carole Kenwright of Chartwell; and, as ever, to Anthea Morton-Saner.

Introduction

Rhetorical power is neither wholly bestowed nor wholly acquired, but cultivated....Every orator means what he says the moment he says it. He may be often inconsistent. He is never consciously insincere.

– Winston S. Churchill

Winston Churchill was not born an orator. He was, however, born with a lisp, which he tried to overcome by rehearsing the phrase, "The Spanish ships I cannot see for they are out of sight." It kept coming out "Schpanish schips" and "schight." Eventually he gave up and turned impediment into asset by accentuating the lisp in his speeches—as in his famous pronunciation of "Nazis" as "Narzhees," a long, gutteral growl.

The loaded pause was Churchill's way of holding an audience.

Some thought Churchill stuttered as well when delivering a speech because of the way he paused, as if searching for a word. But the loaded pause was his way of holding an audience. "Those pauses are just part of my trade," he once confided to an editor friend. "I always—well, most of the time—know exactly what I am going to say, but I make believe, by hesitating a little, that a word or phrase has just come to me. I think the effect is improved."

In 1940 the British people heard quite a lot of those lisps and pauses from their new Prime Minister. But accompanying these devices was a sincerity that was distinctly Churchill's. At the age of 23, in an unpublished essay, "The Scaffolding of Rhetoric" (which is quoted from above), he had stressed the importance of authenticity: "Before the orator can inspire with an emotion, he must be swayed by it himself. When he would rouse [the people's] indignation, his heart is filled with anger. Before he can move their tears, his own must flow. To convince them, he must himself believe."

No speechwriters attended him. Until old age, Churchill wrote every speech himself. To emotion, sincerity and his distinct speaking style, he brought his photographic memory, borrowing freely from Greek and Renaissance philosophers, the Bible, Shakespeare, Victorian poets and nineteenth-century classics.

He committed to memory *Bartlett's Familiar Quotations,* which he used with devastating efficiency.

As a young man he had read every important book on science, philosophy, humanity, government, democracy: "I approached [these learned books] with an empty, hungry mind, and with fairly strong jaws," he wrote in his autobiography, "and what I got I bit." Chewed, digested, pondered and stored in his memory, it was all there like a sort of prehistoric Google, on standby in his mind.

At the age of 20 he read the Parliamentary debates for the past quarter century, deciding what side he would take on each important issue. He committed to memory *Bartlett's Familiar Quotations,* which he used with devastating efficiency. "They that can give up essential liberty to obtain a little temporary safety deserve neither liberty nor safety" is often ascribed to Churchill. But *Bartlett's* records that the first to use this phrase was Benjamin Franklin, in 1755.

Churchill "mobilized the English language and sent it into battle."

In this, his most famous speech, delivered on the 18th of June 1940, Churchill is largely original: "finest hour" and "sunlit uplands" are distinctly his own expressions. But he did deploy lines from the seventeenth-century writer Andrew Marvell:

He nothing common did or mean,
Upon that memorable scene.

John Colville, his private secretary, wrote that Churchill had been repeating this verse to all and sundry since early June.

By the spring of 1940, Western liberty seemed close to extinction. Hitler's German Reich had trammeled most of western Europe. What Hitler hadn't absorbed was closely allied to him—Italy, Hungary, the Soviet Union. Faraway America seemed indifferent, lost in an isolationist dream. Only Great Britain and her Prime Minister, Winston Churchill, stood across Hitler's line of march.

Churchill the orator now took charge. With the Nazis gazing at Dover's cliffs from a mere twenty miles across the English Channel, he "mobilized the English language," as the journalist Edward R. Murrow remarked, "and sent it into battle."

Churchill had not always delivered riveting speeches. In the late 1920s and early 1930s, as he droned on in the House of Commons over the national budget or the future of India, he often spoke to an empty chamber. But he had the ability of rising to the great moment.

"There must be character, personality, delivery, and occasion," he noted. "The wrong man can make the finest phrase ineffective." The war speeches of Churchill's predecessor, Neville Chamberlain, were "like a faint air played on a pipe and lost on the wind," as the novelist A. P. Herbert said, while Churchill's were "like fine tunes."

His purpose on June 18th was to confront the doubters who believed, in the words of one French general, that "in three weeks Britain will have her neck wrung like a chicken." Churchill said: perhaps not. His voice, Herbert recalled, was "like an organ filling the church, and we all went out refreshed and resolute to do or die."

In 1904, as a 30-year-old addressing the House of Commons and relying only on memory, Churchill had once lost his thread; never again did he speak without a text in hand, no matter how well he knew a speech. "The processes of memory and composition are entirely separate in the brain," he wrote, "and it is not easy to change from one gear to the other."

> **As a 30-year-old addressing the House of Commons and relying only on memory, Churchill had once lost his thread; never again did he speak without a text in hand.**

As extraordinary as his stock of words were his methods of preparation: "one hour of prep," he once told his grandson and namesake, "for each minute of delivery." Yet *Finest Hour*, the twenty-nine-minute speech that won him lasting fame, was dictated between Monday evening, June 17th, and noon on the 18th. By rights it should have taken him twenty-nine hours to compose. Clearly it did not, though he had already been composing some of the lines in his mind—as Colville said, for a fortnight—mouthing the words to himself, his wife, his associates, even Nelson the resident cat, as news of the frightening events unfolded.

The Cabinet met at 10 Downing Street from 11 a.m. to 4 p.m. on the 17th. The news was bad: Marshal Pétain, the new head of the French government, had ordered his soldiers to lay down their arms. When the Cabinet adjourned, Churchill strode the garden, bowed in anxious thought, yearning for any kernel of hope amid unremitting disaster. By bedtime the morning newspapers, which he liked to read before retiring, had not arrived. Furious, he upset his weak whisky and soda all over his pile of official dispatches.

> **He had already been composing some of the lines in his mind for a fortnight—mouthing the words to himself, his wife, his associates, even Nelson the cat.**

INTRODUCTION

The morning of the 18th found Churchill dictating to his devoted secretary, Mrs. Kathleen Hill, she using a noiseless typewriter, muffled so no clatter would distract him. The historian David Irving has left a vivid description of the scene at Downing Street:

> His morning work was done a-bed, resplendent in silk kimono….The box of documents sagged open on the coverlet, a silver ice-bucket purloined from the Savoy waited at the bedside to receive the cigar butts. Nelson, the Admiralty's pampered tom, had evicted Chamberlain's black Treasury cat, in the way that felines do to establish their own imperium, and now fondled the new premier's feet….Winston preferred Nelson's company: he found he could converse at any length with cats without fear of interruption, and once he would swear he heard one remark, "These humans are very intelligent: I believe they understand quite a lot of what we say."

The words flowed, Mrs. Hill typing silently, like a court stenographer. Churchill's task was to explain why Britain could hold, having lost most of her arms and equipment in the Dunkirk evacuation, having no ally in arms, having had only promises from Roosevelt, having heard from Moscow only messages congratulating the Germans.

As with all his important speeches, he presented the draft to his wife. She thought it would go down well.

In this portion of the speech there is evidence of much revision. Inwardly Churchill must have wondered: was it too late? In May he had privately confessed his doubts to Roosevelt: he himself would go down fighting, but Britain might be overrun.

But publicly he would say that the Channel was wide, the navy prepared, the army ready. In the last war victory had come from out of the blue. There were reasons to be confident. "It will not be useful to go into details," he added in his own hand.

There were not many details to go into. In an earlier broadcast, having said "we shall fight on the beaches," he had covered the microphone and whispered, "And we will hit them over the heads with beer bottles, which is about all we have got to work with."

> Coincidentally, June 18th, 1940 was the one hundred twenty-fifth anniversary of the victory at Waterloo.

His chief of staff, General Sir Hastings Ismay, wrote in his memoirs that Churchill dictated "without the aid of a note." He certainly had the raw technical data, but his words, Ismay wrote, "came straight from the heart." (Three months later during the London Blitz, Ismay reminded Churchill that whatever happened, he had inspired the country. "Not at all," Churchill snapped back. "It was given to me to express what was in the hearts of the British people.")

The draft complete, Churchill polished until he was satisfied, scribbling corrections in red and blue ink. As with all his important speeches, he presented the draft to his wife, the admirable Clementine—shrewd, practical and a better judge of people than he was. She thought it would go down well.

The corrected text was retyped on smaller sheets the size of notepaper, in what Churchill's secretaries called speech form. They had become adept at this: setting out the phrases as he would deliver them, like blank verse. Lord Halifax, "the Holy Fox," Churchill's religious foreign minister, called it psalm form because it reminded him of lines from the Book of Psalms.

> The corrected text was retyped on smaller sheets in what Churchill's secretaries called speech form: setting out the phrases like blank verse.

The sheets were hole-punched with a tool Churchill called klop, coining the name for the noise it made when in use. (He once told a secretary: "Fetch klop!" She duly hauled out Onno Klopp's fourteen-volume *Der Fall des Hauses Stuart*. "No, you damned fool, give me klop!" If he thought he had wounded a secretary by such outbursts, he would hasten to say, "Good heavens, you mustn't mind me. We're all toads beneath the harrow, you know!")

Klopped and collated, the pages were fastened with a treasury tag—a short piece of yarn with metal bars at each end that allowed him to flip from sheet to sheet while keeping them all together in the proper order. He despised staples or paper clips, which would fall out, leaving him with masses of sheets of paper.

Klopped and collated, the pages were fastened with a treasury tag—he despised staples or paper clips.

At five o'clock on the afternoon of June 18th, Churchill rose to speak in the House of Commons. It was, quite by coincidence, the one hundred twenty-fifth anniversary of the victory at Waterloo.

His colleagues weren't immediately sure how the speech had gone. Colville thought Churchill had spoken less well than on previous occasions but that he had ended magnificently.

The Prime Minister returned to Downing Street and went to bed. It was a habit he had learned years ago, to squeeze a day and a half out of each day: draw the blinds, don pajamas and an eyeshade, say "damn everybody," dive under the covers and sleep soundly for an hour. He would awake refreshed and could then last until three in the morning.

As Churchill was dressing later that evening, Colville brought him a telegram from France. The Pétain government would not move to North Africa to continue the fight in exile. When he saw Colville coming, Churchill anticipated the message that France had capitulated and invoked the World War I slang for death: "Another bloody country gone west, I'll bet."

At 9:00 p.m. at the BBC, Churchill spoke his words again for a radio broadcast. "It was too long and he sounded tired," Colville wrote. "Juliet [Henley, Clementine's cousin] said it was like listening to a bishop. He smoked a cigar the whole time he was broadcasting."

Harold Nicolson, Parliamentary Under-Secretary of State at the Ministry of Information, who heard both orations and thought the Commons version "magnificent," wrote to his wife, Vita Sackville-West, "he hates the microphone, and when we bullied him into speaking he just sulked and read his House of Commons speech all over again….it sounded ghastly on the wireless."

His colleagues weren't immediately sure how the speech had gone. And yet the public took to *Finest Hour* in a way insiders didn't.

And yet the public took to *Finest Hour* in a way insiders didn't. The newspaperman Guy Eden was succinct: "I remember the thrill it caused, that call to battle."

David Low, the newspaper cartoonist, published in the *Evening Standard* a drawing of a soldier resembling the Prime Minister, wearing a steel helmet, standing on the cliffs of Dover and shaking his fist at waves of bombers headed west from the burning continent. The caption was three short words: "Very well, alone!"

When one reads these actual pages of *Finest Hour* today the years roll away, and we hear what the historian David Nichols called "those lisping Churchillian cadences rolling out—that unique delivery midway between poetry and prose."

The Oxford philosopher Isaiah Berlin explained why the speech reverberated. Churchill, he wrote, was neither "a sensitive lens which absorbs and concentrates and reflects and amplifies the sentiments of others," nor a politician who plays on public opinion. Instead, he imposed his own will and determination, imbuing his countrymen "with such intensity that in the end they approached his ideal and began to see themselves as he saw them: 'the buoyant and imperturbable temper of Britain'."

After this speech Churchill was held almost in reverence. The people had never quite trusted him before. He had made his share of mistakes in World War I, fought the labor unions and Gandhi, delivered scary speeches about the "Narzhees," championed Edward VIII in the abdication crisis. And they would turn their backs on him soon enough: the war would not yet be over when they would vote overwhelmingly for his removal. "Ingratitude towards their great men is the mark of strong peoples." Churchill was known to quote these words of Plutarch.

> **After this speech Churchill was held almost in reverence. The people had never quite trusted him before.**

When it mattered, though, Churchill became, in the words of Roosevelt biographer Robert Sherwood, "the living symbol of their will to survive as a free people." After Churchill's June 18th speech, an old RAF flier said of the Germans, "We *wanted* them to come."

When asked for her recollections of the *Finest Hour* speech, Churchill's daughter, Lady Soames, is remarkably disarming. "My information is patchy; I wasn't with him all that much during the war," she says. "But you must remember, speeches were not special occasions for my family. We all knew it was part of Papa's trade, and he got on with it. It was all very routine."

Bibliography

Articles

Churchill, Winston S. "The Scaffolding of Rhetoric." *Finest Hour: Journal of The Churchill Centre and Societies,* no. 94 (Spring 1997): 14-17.

———. "When I 'Dried Up.'" *Pictorial Weekly* (26 May 1934): 16-17.

Nichols, David. "How Churchill Found the Words to Inspire Us." *Saga* (February 2003): 69-75.

Books

Berlin, Isaiah. *Mr. Churchill in 1940.* London: John Murray, 1964.

Cannadine, David, ed. *Blood, Toil, Tears and Sweat: The Speeches of Winston Churchill.* Boston: Houghton Mifflin, 1989.

Charmley, John. *Churchill: The End of Glory: A Political Biography.* Sevenoaks, United Kingdom: Hodder & Stoughton, 1993.

Churchill, Winston S. *My Early Life: A Roving Commission.* London: Thornton Butterworth, 1930.

Churchill, Winston S. *Never Give In! The Best of Winston Churchill's Speeches.* London: Pimlico, 2003.

Colville, John. *Fringes of Power: Downing Street Diaries, 1939-1955.* New York: W. W. Norton, 1985.

Eden, Guy. *Portrait of Churchill.* London and New York: Hutchinson, n.d.

Fishman, Jack. *My Darling Clementine.* New York: MacKay, 1963.

Gardner, Brian. *Churchill in His Time: A Study in a Reputation, 1939-1945.* London: Methuen, 1968.

Gilbert, Martin. *Churchill: A Life.* London: Heinemann, 1991.

———, ed. *The Churchill War Papers.* Vol. II, *Never Surrender, May 1940-December 1940.* London: Heinemann, 1994.

———. *Winston S. Churchill.* Vol. VI, *Finest Hour, 1939-1941.* London: Heinemann, 1983.

Graebner, Walter. *My Dear Mr. Churchill.* Boston: Houghton Mifflin, 1965.

Herbert, A. P. "The Master of Words." In Marchant, James, ed. *Winston Spencer Churchill: Servant of Crown and Commonwealth.* London: Cassell, 1954.

Holley, Darrell. *Churchill's Literary Allusions: An Index to the Education of a Soldier, Statesman and Litterateur.* Jefferson, N.C.: MacFarland, 1987.

Irving, David. *Churchill's War.* Vol. 2, *Triumph in Adversity.* London: Focal Point Publishing, 2001.

Ismay, Hastings. *Memoirs of General the Lord Ismay.* New York: Viking, 1960.

Kimball, Warren F. *Churchill and Roosevelt: The Complete Correspondence.* Vol. I, *Alliance Emerging.* Princeton: Princeton University Press, 1984.

Manchester, William. *The Last Lion: William Spencer Churchill.* Vol. 2, *Alone, 1932-1940.* Boston: Little Brown, 1988.

Nel, Elizabeth. *Mr. Churchill's Secretary.* London: Hodder & Stoughton, 1958.

Nicolson, Nigel, ed. *Harold Nicolson: Diaries and Letters, 1939-1955.* London: Collins, 1967.

Pilpel, Robert. *Churchill in America, 1895-1961: An Affectionate Portrait.* New York: Harcourt Brace Jovanovich, 1976.

Rhodes James, Robert. *The British Revolution, 1880-1939.* New York: Knopf, 1977.

————, ed. *Chips: The Diaries of Sir Henry Channon.* London: Weidenfeld & Nicolson, 1967.

Sherwood, Robert. *Roosevelt and Hopkins.* New York: Harper & Row, 1948.

Taylor, Robert Louis. *Winston Churchill: An Informal Study of Greatness.* Garden City, N.Y.: Doubleday, 1954.

Interviews

Winston S. Churchill (grandson of Sir Winston), Sir John Colville, Ronald Golding, Grace Hamblin, Sir Anthony Montague Browne, Sir Robert Rhodes James, The Lady Soames

Richard M. Langworth is the founder and co-chairman of Trustees of The Churchill Centre (www.winstonchurchill.org) and the editor of its quarterly journal, "Finest Hour." In 1998 he was conferred the title of Commander of the Most Excellent Order of the British Empire (CBE) in honor of his work to preserve the Churchill legacy.

Facsimile
of the
First Draft

I spoke the other day of the colossal

military disaster which occurred when the French High
                        failed
Command ~~neglected~~ to withdraw the Northern armies from

Belgium at the moment when they knew that the French

Front was decisively broken at Sedan and on the Meuse.
                                        two fifteen or sixteen
This delay entailed the loss of ~~at least fifteen~~ French

Divisions and threw out of action for the critical period
                                        and 120,000 French troops
the whole British Expeditionary Force. Our Army/~~indeed~~
        have escaped to her   they   *these*
no doubt ~~escaped~~, but with the loss of all ~~its~~ cannon, vehicles
            modern
and/equipment. This inevitably took some weeks to repair,
        the first line of
and in those weeks the ~~great~~ battle of France has been

lost. When we consider the heroic resistance made by the
                    heavy
French Army at ~~enormous~~ odds in this battle, and the
    enormous   *evident*
~~enormous~~ losses inflicted upon the enemy, and the exhaustion

of the enemy, it may well be thought that those twenty-five

Divisions of the best troops might have turned the scale.

However General Weygand had to fight without them. Only

~~the equiv~~ two British Divisions or their equivalent were

we could no doubt rescued by the Royal Navy

able to stand in the line with their French comrades .
They have suffered heavily, but they have fought well.
We sent every man we could to France as fast as we could
re-equip ~~them~~ and transport their formations, ~~the-~~ I am
not reciting these facts for any purpose of recrimination.
That I judge to be utterly futile and ~~even harmful~~ even harmful. I
recite them in order to explain why it was we did not have,
as we could have had, about fourteen British ~~Divisons~~ Divisions
fighting in the Line ~~instead of only two~~ during this great
battle instead of only two.   Now I put this all aside. I
put it on the shelf from which historians will select their
documents to tell their stories. We have to think of the
future and not of the past.

This also applies in a small way to our own
affairs at home. There are many who wish to hold an inquest
upon the conduct of the Governments and of the Parliaments -
for they are in it too - during the years which led up to
this catastrophe. They ~~wish~~ seek to indict those who

were responsible for the guidance of our affairs. This

foolish

also would be a ~~futile~~ and pernicious process. There

are too many in it. Let each man search his conscience.

I frequently search mine. Of this I am sure; ~~If we set~~

~~up a tribunal~~ open a quarrel between the past and the

present, we shall find that we have lost the future.

Therefore I cannot ~~allow any~~ accept the drawing of any

distinction between Members of the present Government. It

was formed at a moment of crisis, it has received the

almost unanimous support of both Houses of Parliament,

its Members are going to stand together and we are

going to ~~given~~ govern. It is ~~essential~~ absolutely

necessary at a time like this that every Minister who

tries each day to do his duty shall be respected ~~and obeyed~~,

and ~~that~~ their subordinates ~~shall~~ know that they are not

men who are here today and gone tomorrow, but that their

directions must be obeyed.

5

The military events which have
happened in France during the last fortnight have
not come to me with any sense of surprise. Indeed I
indicated as clearly as I could to the House that the
worst possibilities were open, and I made it perfectly
clear then that whatever happened in France would make
no difference to ~~our~~ the resolve of Britain and the British
Empire to fight on if necessary for years , if necessary
alone. During the last few days we have successfully
brought off the great ~~mass~~ majority of the troops we had on the
line, of communication, and seven-eighths of all the
troops we have sent to France since the beginning of
the war - that is to say about 350,000 men are safely
back in this country. Others are still fighting with
the French. We have also brought back a great mass of
~~stores~~/and ~~ammunition~~ rifles munitions of all kinds which had been
accumulated in France during the last nine months. We
have therefore in this ~~country~~ Island today a very large and
powerful military force. This force includes all our

Those who are not called up or employed upon the vast business of munitions production in all its branches would serve the country best by remaining at their ordinary work until they are required.

best-trained and finest troops, including ~~those~~ scores

of thousands of those who have already measured their

~~strength~~ *quality* against the Germans and found themselves at

no disadvantage. We have under arms at the present time

over ~~1,500,000~~ *a million and a quarter* men, behind these we have the Local

Defence Volunteers, numbering half a million, only a

portion of whom, however, are yet armed with rifles or

other firearms. We have incorporated into our defence *forces*

every man for whom we have a weapon. We expect very large

additions to our weapons in the near future, and in

preparation for ~~these~~ *this* we intend to call up, drill and

train further large numbers. We have also here the

Australian and Canadian Armies, the Canadians had actually

landed in France but have now been safely withdrawn *(much disappointed but in perfect order)* with

all their artillery and equipment, and both these very

high-class forces from the Dominions will now take part

in the defence of the Mother Country. Lest the account

I have given of these very large forces should raise the

question why they did not intervene in the battle in

a million and a quarter

Those who are not called up or employed upon the vast business of munitions production in all its branches would serve the country best by remaining at their ordinary work, and also until they are required.

New para

Apart from the [divisions] trained & organised units of the Home Defence ... for Home Defence

led to expect will be available for these 60 ...units ... the war.

on a basis suitable for

France, I must make it clear that only fourteen Divisions

were equipped upon a scale which justified their being

and these was fully up to the number which the French had been ... own force

sent abroad, ~~Although those who remaine~~ the rest have a

apart from 4 divisions trained & organised upon a basis suitable for Home Defence,

high fighting value for home defence. ~~This value~~ *which will* of course

will steadily increase with every ~~month~~ *week* that passes.   Thus

the invasion of Great Britain would at this time require

                              hostile
the transport across the sea of/armies on a very large scale,

and after they had been transported they would have to be

continually maintained with all the immense mass of munitions

and supplies which are required for continuous battle. *the* ⟨Now

                    After all we have a Navy.
here is where we come to the Navy./ For more than thirty

and this was fully up to the number which French born be led to expect would be available ... the number for several months ... month of ... the well)

years I have been concerned in discussions about the

possibilities of an over-sea invasion, and I took the

responsibility at the beginning of the last war of allowing

all the regular troops to be sent out of the country, although

our territorials had only just been called up and were quite

untrained, and ~~therefore~~ this ~~country~~ Island was ~~... then ...~~

                    ... fighting fighting
practically denuded of troops. So great was ~~the~~ ~~consequence~~ *confidence*

                    had confidence
of ~~the~~ Admiralty at that time in their ability to prevent a

mass invasion, even though ~~at that time~~ the Germans had a

magnificent battle-fleet, in the proportion of ten to sixteen

and capable of fighting ^a general^ battle any day, whereas now

they have only two heavy ships worth speaking of. Therefore

it seems to me that so far as sea-borne invasion is concerned ^on a great scale^

we are ~~in far less danger~~ ^far more capable of meeting it^ today than we were at many periods

in the last war, and during the early months of this war,

before our other troops were trained and while the British

Expeditionary Force were still abroad. / ~~Now~~ the Navy have

never pretended to be able to prevent raids by bodies of

five or ten thousand men flung ^suddenly^ ~~hastily~~ acfoss and thrown

ashore at several points of the coast some dark night or

foggy morning .

9

The efficacy of sea power, especially
depends upon the
under modern conditions, ~~requires that the mass of the~~
being
invading force ~~shall be~~ of a large size, so that the

Navy have something to bite on, and something they can

find and meet.   Now even five Divisions very lightly

equipped would require 200 to 250 ships, and with the

modern Air reconnaissance and photography, it would not

be easy to collect such an armada, marshal it, and conduct

it across the sea, without any powerful naval force to

escort it, without very great ~~danger~~ possibilities that

it would be intercepted long before it reached the coast,

and the men all drowned in the sea, or at the worst,

(with their equipment)

~~blown to pieces as they landed~~ while they were trying

to land.   We have also a great system of minefields,
recently largely reinforced,
~~some of which have been declared,~~ and through which we
If the enemy tries to sweep passages through these minefields
alone know the channels.   The question is whether there

are any new methods by which these solid assurances can

be circumvented. Odd as it may seem, some attention has

been given to this, by the Admiralty, whose first duty

and responsibility it is to destroy any large sea-borne

[left margin handwritten:] If the enemy tries to sweep passages through these minefields it will be the task of the Navy to destroy the minesweepers & any other force employed to protect them. There ought to be no difficulty in this owing to our great superiority at sea. it will be the task of the Navy to destroy the minesweepers & any other force

[bottom handwritten:] employed to protect them. There ought to be no difficulty in this owing to our great superiority at sea.

expedition before it reaches, or at the moment it reaches, these shores. *It will not be useful to go into details. All I will say is that the unceasing vigilance & mind searching must be devoted to the subject because the enemy is crafty & full of novel treachery & stratagems.*

11

Some people will ask why then was it that

the British Navy was not able to prevent the movement

of a large army from Germany into Norway across the

Skagerrak.   But the conditions in the Channel and

the North Sea in no way resemble those which prevail

in the Skagerrak.   In the Skagerrak we could give no

Air protection to our surface ships, and were compelled

to use only our submarines.   These took a heavy toll, but

could not prevent the invasion of Norway by themselves.

In the Channel and the North Sea, on the other hand, our

superior naval surface forces, aided by our submarines

will operate under effective Air protection.

This brings me naturally to the great question

of invasion from the Air, and of the impending struggle

between the British and German Air Forces.   It seems quite

clear that no very-large invasion on a scale which cannot

be dealt with by our land forces to crush speedily, is

likely to take place until our Air Force has been definitely

overpowered.   In the meantime, there may be raids by

parachute troops and attempted landin- descents by

air-borne soldiers.   We ought to be able to give these

people a warm reception, both in the Air, and if they reach

the ground in any condition to continue the dispute.

But the great question is, can we break Hitler's Air weapon?

have not got

Now of course it is a very great pity that we ~~did not have~~

the

an Air Force at least equal to that of ~~our~~ most powerful

enemy within reach of our shores.   But we have a very

powerful Air Force which has proved itself far superior in

many types of

quality, both of men and machines, to what we have met so far

in the numerous, fierce Air battles which have been fought

~~in the fighting over Dunkirk, which was a sort of~~

in France, where we were at a considerable disadvantage,

We were accustomed to inflict a loss of 2 to 2½ to 1

In the fighting over Dunkirk, which was a sort of no man's

land, we undoubtedly beat the German Air Force and ~~became~~

~~mast~~   gained the mastery of the local Air, ~~we~~ inflicting

a loss of 3 or 4 to 1 .   Anyone who looked at the photographs

of the re-embarkation showing the masses of troops assembled

on the beaches of perfect target for hours at a time must

realise that ~~the en~~ this would not have been impossible

unless the enemy had resigned all hope of recovering Air
superiority.   In the defence of this Island, the advantages
of the defenders will be very great.   We hope to improve
upon the rate of 3 or 4 to 1, which was realised at Dunkirk,
and in addition all the injured machines and their crews
which get down safely, of which there are a great many in
Air fighting, fall on to friendly soil and live to fight
another day, whereas all injured enemy machines and their
complements will be total losses.   [N.P. During the great battle
in France, we gave very powerful continuous aid to the French
Army, both by fighters and bombers, but in spite of every
kind of pressure, we never would allow the entire strength
of the metropolitan strength of the Air Force in fighters
to be consumed.   This decision was painful, but it was also
right, because the fortunes of the battle in France could
not have been decisively affected, even if we had thrown
in our entire Air fighter force.   That battle was lost by
the unfortunate strategic opening by the extraordinary
unforeseen power of the armoured columns, and by the very
great German preponderance in numbers.   Our fighter Air
Force might easily have been exhausted as a mere incident
in the struggle, and we should have found ourselves at the

present time in a very serious plight. As it is, I am
happy to inform the House that our Fighter Air strength
is stronger at the present time ~~actually, and still more~~
relatively to the Germans who have suffered terrible
losses, than it has ever been, and that consequently we
believe ourselves possessed of the capacity to continue
the war in the Air under better conditions than we have
ever experienced before.   I look forward confidently to
the exploits of our fighter pilots who will have the
glory of saving their native land, their Island home,
and all they love, from the most deadly of all attacks.

There remains the danger of the ~~he~~ bombing
attacks which will certainly be made very soon upon us
by the ~~superior~~ bomber force of the enemy. It is quite
true that this force is superior in numbers to ours, and
by ~~coming on dark nights they may inflict grievous damage
without the certainty of being intercepted.~~ But we have
a very large bombing force also, which we shall use to
strike at military targets in Germany without intermission.

15

I do not at all underrate the severity of the ordeal which lies before us, but I believe our countrymen will show themselves capable of standing up to it, and carrying on in spite of it, at least as well as any other people in the world. Much will depend on this, and every man and woman will have the chance to show the finest qualities of their race, and to render the highest service to their cause.For all of us whatever our sphere or station it will be a help to remember Marvell's famous lines: 'He did nothing common did or mean upon that memorable scene.'

16

I have thought it right on this occasion
to ent- give the House and the country some indication
of the solid gre practical grounds upon which we base
our inflexible resolve to continue the war, and I can
assure them that in-the-opinion-of our professional
advisers of the three Services unitedly advise that
we should do so, and that there are good and reasonable
hopes of final victory.

We may now ask ourselves in what way ~~is~~ has our

position worsened since the beginning of the war. It is

worsened by the fact that the Germans have conquered a

large part of the coastline of Western Europe, and many

small countries have been overrun by them. This aggravates

the possibilities of Air attack, and ~~to some extent~~ adds

to our naval preoccupations It in no way diminishes, but

on the contrary definitely increases the power of our long-

distance blockade. Should military resistance come to an

end in France, which is not yet certain, ~~and~~ though it will in any

case be greatly diminished, the Germans can concentrate

their forces, ~~upon us.~~ both military and industrial, upon us.

But for the reasons I have given to the House, these will

not be found ~~so~~ easy to apply, ~~and certainly not to apply~~

~~immediately.~~ If invasion becomes more imminent, we being

relieved from the task of maintaining a large army in France

have far larger and more sufficient forces here to meet it.

If Hitler can bring under his despotic control the industries

of the countries he has conquered, this will add greatly to

his already vast armament output. On the other hand, this

will not happen immediately, and we are now assured
of immense continuous support in supplies and munitions
of all kinds from the United States, and especially of
aeroplanes and pilots from the Dominions and across the
oceans, who will come from regions outside the reach of
enemy bombers.   I do not see how any of these factors
can operate to our detriment on the balance before the
winter comes, and the winter will impose a strain upon the
Nazi regime, with half Europe writhing and starving under
its heel, which for all their ruthlessness will run them
very hard.

19

We must ~~never~~ not forget that from the moment

that we declared war on the 3rd September, it was always

possible for Germany to turn all her Air Force upon this

country, together with any other devices of invasion, and

that France could do little or nothing to prevent ~~this~~ her.

We have therefore lived under this danger during all these

months.   In the meanwhile, however, we have enormously

improved our methods of defence, and we have learned what

we had no right to assume at the beginning, of the individual

superiority of our aircraft and pilots.   Therefore in

casting up this dread balance sheet, and contemplating

~~all the~~ our dangers with a disillusioned eye, I see

great reason for intense exertion and vigilance, but none

whatever for panic or despair. ~~or despondency.~~

During the first four years of the last War

the Allies
~~we~~ experienced nothing but disaster and disappointment,

and yet at the end their morale was higher than that of

the Germans who had moved from one aggressive triumph to

another.   During that War, we repeatedly asked ourselves

the question, how are we going to win?

and no one was ever able to answer it with much c̶o̶n̶f̶i̶d̶e̶n̶c̶e̶/

precision, until at the end, quite suddenly and unexpectedly,

our terrible foes collapsed before us, and we were so

glutted t̶h̶a̶-̶-̶i̶n̶ ^with victory that in our folly we threw it away.

We do not know yet what will happen in
France, or whether the French resistance will be prolonged
both in France and in the French Empire overseas. The
French Government will be throwing away great opportunities
~~and turning from their duty~~ if they do not continue the
war in accordance with their Treaty obligations from which
we have not felt able to release them. The House will
have read the historic ~~declaration~~ declaration in which
at the desire of many Frenchmen, and of our own hearts,
we have proclaimed our willingness to conclude at the
darkest hour in French history, ~~an indissoluble~~ a Union
However matters may go in France, or with the French
Government, we in this Island and in the British Empire,
will never lose our sense of comradeship with the French
people. If we are now called upon to endure ~~their~~
~~sufferings, and to fight on alone~~, and if final victory
rewards our ~~efforts~~ toils, they shall share the gain,
aye, and freedom shall be restored to all. ~~While~~ Czechs,
Poles, Norwegians, ~~Danish~~ Dutch and Belgians, who have
joined their causes with our own.

~~The~~ battle of France is over

What General Weygand calls 'the battle of
France' is over. The battle of Britain is about to begin.
Upon this battle depends the survival of Christian
civilisation. Upon it depends our own British life and
the long continuity of our institutions, and our Empire.
The whole fury and might of the enemy must very soon be
turned on us. Hitler knows that ~~if~~ he will have to break
us in this Island, or lose the war. If we can stand up
to him, all Europe may be liberated, and the life of the
world may move forward into broad and sunlit uplands.
But if we fail, then the whole world, including the United
States, and all that we have known and cared for, will
sink into the abyss of a new Dark Age made more sinister
by the lights of perverted Science. Let us therefore
brace ourselves to our duty, and so bear ourselves that
if the British Empire and Commonwealth lasts for a thousand
years, men will still say,'This was their finest hour.'

Facsimile
of the
Final Draft

I spoke the other day of the colossal
military disaster which occurred
when the French High Command
failed to withdraw the Northern
armies
from Belgium at the moment
when they knew that the French
Front
was decisively broken
at Sedan and on the Meuse.

This delay entailed the loss of
fifteen or sixteen French Divisions

and threw out of action for the
critical period

the whole B.E.F.

Our Army and 120,000 French troops
were no doubt rescued by the British
Navy
but with the loss of all their cannon,
vehicles & modern equipment.

This inevitably took some weeks to
repair,
and in the first two of those weeks
the battle of France has bn lost.

When we consider the heroic resistance
made by the French Army at heavy odds
in this battle,
and the enormous losses inflicted
upon the enemy,
and the evident exhaustion of the
enemy,
it may well be thought that those
25 Divisions of the best troops might
hv turned the scale.

2

However General Weygand had to fight
                    without them.

Only 3 Br: Divisions
    or their equivalent
        were able to stand in the line
                with their French comrades.

They hv suffered heavily,

    but they have fought well.

We sent every man we could to France
    as fast as we could re-equip and
            transport their formations.

I am not reciting these facts for any
    purpose of recrimination.

    That I judge to be utterly futile
                and even harmful.

I recite them in order to explain why
    it was we did not have, as we cd hv
                            had,
    between about 14 Br: Divisions fighting in
        the line during this great battle

        instead of only 3.

Now I put all this aside.

I put it on the shelf from which
    historians will select their documents
            to tell their stories.

3

We hv to think of the future
  and not of the past.

This also applies in a small way
  to our own affairs at home.

There are many who wish to hold an
                        inquest
    upon the conduct of the Governments,
      and of the Parliaments - for they
                    are in it too -

    during the years which led up to this
                        catastrophe.

They seek to indict those who were
    responsible for the guidance of our
                        affairs.

This also would be a foolish and
                pernicious process.

There are too many in it.

Let each man search his conscience.

    I frequently search mine.

Of this I am sure;

    if we open a quarrel between the past
                    and the present,

    we shall find that we hv lost the
                        future.

Therefore I cannot accept the drawing of
    any distinction between Members of the
                present Government.

4

It was formed at a moment of crisis in
   order to unite all the Parties and all
      sections of opinion.

It has received the almost unanimous
   support of both Houses of Parliament.

Its Members are going to stand together
   and subject to the authority of the H/C
   we are going to govern the country
      and fight the war.

It is absolutely necessary at a time
                              like this
   that every Minister who tries each day
      to do his duty
         shall be respected,

and their subordinates must know
   that their chiefs are not threatened
                              men -

   men who are here today and gone
                        tomorrow -

   but that their directions must be
                        obeyed.

Without this concentrated power
   we cannot face what lies before us.

*Scual Sensw of Thing,: us now fulmy that
                         whal a unal a unula*

The military events which hv happened
   in France during the last fortnight hv
      not come to me with any sense of
                           surprise.

Indeed I indicated as clearly as I could
to the House that the worst
             possibilities were open,

and I made it perfectly clear then
that whatever happened in France

      would make no difference to the
      resolve of Britain and the
      British Empire to fight on -

"if necessary for years,
      if necessary alone."

During the last few days we hv
successfully brought off the great
   majority of the troops we had on the
   lines of communication in France,

and seven-eighths of all the troops
we hv sent to France since the
beginning of the war -

that is to say about 350,000 out of
400,000 men are safely back in this
           country.

Others are still fighting with the
          French.

We hv also brought back a great mass
of stores, rifles and munitions of all
          kinds
which had bn accumulated in France
during the last nine months.

6

We hv therefore in this Island today a
  very large and powerful military force.

This force includes all our best-trained
            and finest troops,

      including scores of thousands of
        those who hv already measured their
        quality against the Germans

      and found themselves at no
                        disadvantage.

We hv under arms at the present time
  over a million and a quarter men,

      behind these we have the Local Defence
                        Volunteers,
        numbering half a million,

      only a portion of whom, however,

      are yet armed with rifles or other
                        firearms.

We hv incorporated into our defence
                        forces
  every man for whom we hv a weapon.

We expect very large additions to our
  weapons in the near future,

      and in preparation for this we intend
        to call up, drill and train further
                        large numbers.

7

Those who are not called up, or employed

upon the vast business of munitions
production in all its branches wd
serve the country best by remaining
at their ordinary work until they
are required.

We hv also here the Australian and
Canadian armies.

The Canadians had actually landed in
France but hv now been safely
withdrawn,

much disappointed but in perfect
order
with all their artillery & equipment,

and both these very high-class forces
from the Dominions will now take
part in the defence of the
Mother Country.

Lest the account I hv given of these
very large forces shd raise the
question why they did not intervene
in the battle in France,

I must make it clear that,
apart from the divisions training
and organising at Home,
only 12 Divisions were equipped
to fight upon a scale which
justified their being sent abroad,

and this was fully up to the number
which the French had been led to
expect wd be available at the
ninth month of the war.

The rest of our force has a fighting
value for home defence which will,
of course, steadily increase
with every week that passes.

Thus the invasion of Gt.Britain wd at
this time require the transport*ation*
across the sea of hostile armies
on a very large scale,

and after they had bn transported
they wd hv to be continually
maintained with all the immense
mass of munitions and supplies
which are required
for continuous battle.

as continuous battle it will be

=

Now here is where we come to the Navy.

After all we hv a Navy.

For more than 30 yrs. I hv bn concerned
in discussions about the possibilities
of an over-sea invasion,

and I took the responsibility *on behalf of his government*
at the beginning of the last war

of allowing all the Regular Troops
to be sent out of the country,

although our Territorials had only
just been called up
and were quite untrained.

Therefore this island was for several
months practically denuded of
fighting troops.

The Admiralty had confidence at that
time in their ability to prevent
a mass invasion,

even though the Germans then had a
magnificent battle-fleet,

in the proportion of ten to sixteen
and capable of fighting a general
engagement ~~battle~~ any day,

whereas now they hv only two
heavy ships worth speaking of.

Therefore it seems to me that so far
as sea-borne invasion on a great scale
in concerned,

we are far more capable of
meeting it today than we were
at many periods in the last
war,
and during the early months of this
war, before our other troops were
trained and while the B.E.F.
were still abroad.

10

The Navy hv never pretended to be able to
prevent raids by bodies of five or
ten thousand men
flung suddenly across and thrown
ashore at several points of
the coast some dark night
or foggy morning.

The effi̶c̶i̶e̶n̶c̶y *acy.* of sea power,
especially under modern conditions,

depends upon the invading force
being of a large size,

that the Navy hv s̶o̶m̶e̶t̶h̶i̶n̶g̶ ̶t̶o̶
b̶i̶t̶e̶ ̶o̶n̶,

and something they can find and meet.
a as it were — to bite on.
Now even five Divisions very lightly
equipped would require 200 to 250
ships,

and with the modern Air
reconnaissance and photography

it would not be easy to collect such
an armada, marshal it, and conduot
it across the sea,

without any powerful naval force
to escort it;
And them will be
-̶w̶i̶t̶h̶o̶u̶t̶ very great possibilities
that it would be intercepted
long before it reached the
coast,

and the men all drowned in the sea,
or at the worst, blown to pieces
with their equipment while they
were trying to land.

11

We hv also a great system of mine-
                                                  fields,
    recently ~~largely~~ reinforced,

      through which we alone know the
                         channels.

If the enemy tries to sweep passages
    through these minefields it will be
      the task of the Navy to destroy
        the minesweepers and any other
          force employed to protect
                    them.

There ought to be no difficulty in
    this owing to our great superiority
                   at sea.

The question is whether there are any
    new methods by which these solid
       assurances can be circumvented.

Odd as it may seem,
    some attention has been given to
       this by the Admiralty,

    whose ~~first~~ former duty and responsibility
    it is to destroy any large
      sea-borne expedition before it
      reaches,
        or at the moment it reaches,
              these shores.

It would not be useful to go into
               details.

All I will say is that untiring
    vigilance and mind-searching must be
    devoted to the subject because the
      enemy is crafty, cunning and
        full of novel treacheries
        and stratagems.

12

Some people will ask
    why then was it tt the Br. Navy
        was not able to prevent the movement
            of a large army from G.
                into Norway across the
                                    Skagerrak.

But the conditions in the Channel and
                            North Sea
        in no way resemble those which prevaile⟩
                    in the Skagerrak.

In the Skagerrak we cd give no Air support
        to our surface ships,
        and (going down in waters close to the enemy's main air
        and were compelled to use only our ⟍ know
                                    submarines.

These took a heavy toll,
        but cd not prevent the invasion
            of Norway by themselves.

In the Channel and the North Sea,
        on the other hand,

        our superior naval surface forces,
            aided by our submarines
                will operate w close and effective
                            Air assistance.

13

This brings me naturally to great question
of invasion from the Air,

and of impending struggle
between the Br. and G. Air Forces.

It seems quite clear tt no invasion
on a scale beyond capacity of our land
forces to crush speedily,

is likely to take place
until our Air Force has bn definitely
overpowered.

In the meantime, there may be raids by
parachute troops,
and attempted descents by air-borne
soldiers.

We ought to be able to give these gently people
a warm reception,
both in the Air,
and if they reach the ground
in any condition to continue the
dispute.

But the great question is,
can we break Hitler's Air weapon?

Now of course it is a very great pity
tt we have not got an Air Force
at least equal to tt
of the most powerful enemy
within reach of our shores.

But we have a vy powerful Air Force
which has proved itself
far superior in quality,
both of men and many types of
machines,
to what we have met so far
in the numerous, fierce Air battles
which have been fought.

14

In France, where we were at a considerable
                                        disadvantage,
        we were accustomed to inflict
            a loss of 2 to 2½ to one.

In the fighting over Dunkirk,
        which was a sort of no man's land,

            we undoubtedly beat the G. Air Force
                and gained mastery of the local Air,
                    inflicting a loss of 3 or 4
                                            to one.

Anyone who looked at the photographs
        of the re-embarkation,
            showing the masses of troops
                assembled on the beaches,
                    forming a perfect target
                        for hours at a time,

            must realise tt this wd not have been
                                            possible
                unless the enemy had resigned all hope
                    of recovering Air superiority.

In the defence of this Island,
        the advantages of the defenders
            will be vy great.

We hope to improve upon the rate
        of 3 or 4 to one, which was realised at
                                        Dunkirk,
            and in addition, all injured machines
                and their crews which get down safely,

            of which there are a great many
                                in Air fighting,

            fall on to friendly soil
                and live to fight another day,

            whereas all injured enemy machines
                and their complements will be total
                                            losses.

During the great battle in France,
    we gave vy powerful continuous aid
        to the French Army,
            both by fighters and bombers,

    but in spite of every kind of pressure,
    we never wd allow the entire
        metropolitan strength
            of the Air Force in fighters
                to be consumed.

This decision was painful,
    but it was also right,

        because the fortunes of the battle in
                            France
        cd not have been decisively affected,
            even if we had thrown in
                our entire Air fighter force.

That battle was lost
    by the unfortunate strategic opening,

        by the extraordinary unforeseen power
                    of the armoured columns,

        and by the vy great G. preponderance
                        in numbers.

Our fighter Air Force might easily
    have been exhausted
        as a mere incident in the struggle,

        and we shd hv found ourselves
        at the present time in a vy serious
                            plight.

As it is, I am happy to inform the House
tt our Fighter Air strength
        is stronger at present time relatively
            to the Germans, who have suffered
                    terrible losses,
        than it has ever been,

    and tt consequently we believe ourselves
        possessed of the capacity
            to continue the war in the Air
                under better conditions

            than we have ever experienced
                    before.

I look forward confidently
    to the exploits of our fighter pilots
        who will have the glory
            of saving their native land,

        their Island home, and all they love,
            from the most deadly
                    of all attacks.

There remains the danger of the bombing
                        attacks
        which will certainly be made very soon
            upon us by the bomber forces
                    of the enemy.

It is quite true that this force
    is superior in numbers to ours.

But we have a very large bombing force
                        also,

    which we shall use
        to strike at military targets in G.
                without intermission.

I do not at all underrate
  the severity of the ordeal
    which lies before us,

  but I believe our countrymen
    will show themselves capable
      of standing up to it,

    and carrying on in spite of it,
      at least as well as any other
        people in the world.

Much will depend on this,
  and every man and woman
    will have the chance to show
      the finest qualities of their race

  and to render the highest service
                to their cause.

For all of us, whatever our sphere or
                        station,
    it will be a help
      to remember Marvell's famous lines:

      'He nothing common did or mean

      Upon that memorable scene'.

I hv thought it right on this occasion
  to give the House and the country
    some indication of the solid,practical
                                    grounds
      upon which we base our inflexible
        resolve to continue the war,

    and I can assure them
      tt our professional advisers
        of the three Services

      unitedly advise tt we shd do so,

    and tt there are good and reasonable
        hopes of final victory.

We have fully informed and consulted
  all the self-governing Dominions,

    and I have received from their P.Ms.,
      Mr. Mackenzie King, Mr. Menzies,
        Mr. Fraser, and General Smuts,

      messages couched in the most moving
                                    terms

      in which they endorse our decision
        and declare themselves ready
          to share our fortunes, and to
            persevere to the end.

We may now ask ourselves in what way
  has our position worsened
        since the beginning of the war.

It is worsened by the fact
    tt the Gs have conquered a large part
        of the coastline of Western Europe,

    and many small countries
        hv bn overrun by them.

This aggravates the possibilities of Air
                                attack,
        and adds to our naval preoccupations.

It in no way diminishes,
    but on the contrary definitely increases
        the power of our long-distance
                            blockade.

Should military resistance come to an end
                        in France,
    which is not yet certain,
    (though it will in any case
        be greatly diminished,)

    the Germans can concentrate their forces,
        both military and industrial,
                        upon us.

But for the reasons I have given to House,
    these will not be found easy to apply.

If invasion becomes more imminent,
    we, being relieved from the task
        of maintaining a large army in France,
            have far larger and more efficient
                forces here to meet it.

If Hitler can bring under his despotic
                        control
the industries of the countries he has
                       conquered,

  this will add greatly
    to his already vast armament output.

On the other hand, this will not happen
                   immediately,
  and we are now assured
    of immense continuous support
    in supplies and munitions
      of all kinds from the United
                States,

    and especially of aeroplanes and pilots
     from the Dominions and across the
                 oceans

    who will come from regions
      outside the reach of enemy bombers

I do not see how any of these factors
  can operate to our detriment
    on the balance before the winter comes

  and the winter will impose a strain
    upon the Nazi regime,

    with ~~half~~ all-Europe writhing
     and starving under its heel,

  which, for all their ruthlessness,
    will run them very hard.

21

We must not forget that from the moment
tt we declared war on Sept: 3,
it was always possible for Germany
to turn all her Air Force upon
this country,
together with any other devices of
invasion,
and tt France cd do little or nothing
to prevent her.

We have therefore lived under this
danger during all these months.

In the meanwhile, however, we hv
enormously improved our methods of
defence, and we hv learned what
we had no right to assume at
the beginning,
of the individual
superiority of our aircraft
and pilots.

Therefore in casting up this dread
balance sheet,
and contemplating our dangers
with a disillusioned eye,

I see great reason for intense
exertion and vigilance,
but none whatever for panic or
despair.

22

During the 1st 4 yrs. of the last war
the Allies experienced nothing
but disaster and disappointment,
and yet at the end their morale
was higher than that of the
Germans who had moved from
one aggressive triumph to
another.

During that War, we repeatedly asked
ourselves the question,

how are we going to win?

And no one was ever able to answer it
with much precision,
until at the end,
quite suddenly & unexpectedly

our terrible foe collapsed before us,

and we were so glutted with victory
that in our folly we threw it away.

We do not know yet what will happen
in France,
or whether the French resistance
will be prolonged both in France
and in the French Empire
overseas.

The French Govt. will be throwing away
great opportunities and casting away
their future if they do not
continue the war in accordance
with their Treaty obligations from
which we hv not felt able to
release them.

23

The House will hv read the historic
  declaration in which at the desire
    of many Frenchmen,
        and of our own hearts,
            we hv proclaimed our willingness
              to conclude at the darkest
                hour in French history,
              a Union of common
                  citizenship in their
                          struggle.

However matters may go in France,
  or with the French Govt.
    we in this Island and in the
      British Empire,
          will never lose our sense of
            comradeship with the French
                        people.

If we are now called upon to endure
  what they hv suffered,
    we shall emulate their courage,
      and if final victory rewards our
                            toils,
          they shall share the gain,____
            aye, and freedom shall be
                restored to all.

We abate nothing of our just demands.

Czechs, Poles, Norwegians, Dutch and
    Belgians, who have joined their
            causes with our own.
          All shall be restored,
What General Weygand calls 'the battle
  of France' is over.

The battle of Britain is about to
                      begin.

Upon this battle depends the
  survival of Christian civilization.

Upon it depends our own British life
 and the long continuity of our
  institutions, and our Empire.

The whole fury and might of the enemy
 must very soon be turned on us.

Hitler knows that he will hv to break
 us in this Island, or lose the war.

If we can stand up to him,
   all Europe may be freed,
    and the life of the world
     may move forward into the
      broad and sunlit uplands.

But if we fail,
  then the whole world,
    including the United States,
     and all that we have known and
             cared for,
     will sink into the abyss of a
     new Dark Age
       made more sinister and
        perhaps more prolonged by
        the lights of perverted
         Science.

Let us therefore brace ourselves to
  our duty, and so bear ourselves that
   if the British Empire and
    Commonwealth lasts for a
     thousand years, men will still
     say,

   'This was their finest hour'.

Uncommon Books
for Serious Readers

Boston
Henry Cabot Lodge

The Dream
Sir Winston Churchill

Feeding the Mind
Lewis Carroll

A Fortnight in the Wilderness
Alexis de Tocqueville

The Little Guide to Your
Well-Read Life
Steve Leveen

The Making of The Finest Hour
Speech by Winston S. Churchill
Introduction by Richard M. Langworth

New York
Theodore Roosevelt

On a Life Well Spent
Cicero
Preface by Benjamin Franklin

Painting as a Pastime
Winston S. Churchill

Samuel Johnson's Dictionary
Selections from the 1755 work
that defined the English language
Edited by Jack Lynch

Samuel Johnson's Insults
Edited by Jack Lynch

The Silverado Squatters
Six selected chapters
Robert Louis Stevenson

Sir Winston Churchill's Life
Through His Paintings
David Coombs
with Minnie Churchill
Foreword by Mary Soames

Levenger Press is the publishing arm of

LEVENGER®
TOOLS FOR SERIOUS READERS

Levenger.com   800.544.0880

Visit our online literary community
wellreadlife.com

XI.

air-borne soldiers.   We ought to be able to give these
people a warm reception, both in the Air, and if they reach
the ground in any condition to continue the dispute.

But the great question is, can we break Hitler's Air weapon?
                                                    have not got
Now of course it is a very great pity that we did not have
                                                        the
an Air Force at least equal to that of our most powerful

powerful Air Force which has proved itself far super
                        many types of
quality, both of men and machines, to what we hav
            in the numerous, fierce Air bat
                in the fig